Who Was
Alex Trebek?

by Pam Pollack and Meg Belviso

illustrated by Ted Hammond

Penguin Workshop

For Pete Freedberger—PP

To Joan "Don't call me when
Jeopardy's on" Belviso—MB

To Mom—TH

PENGUIN WORKSHOP
An imprint of Penguin Random House LLC, New York

First published in the United States of America by Penguin Workshop,
an imprint of Penguin Random House LLC, New York, 2022

Visit us online at penguinrandomhouse.com.

Library of Congress Control Number: 2022032755

Printed in the United States of America

ISBN 9780593383711 (paperback)   10 9 8 7 6 5 4 3 2 1 WOR
ISBN 9780593383728 (library binding)   10 9 8 7 6 5 4 3 2 1 WOR

Contents

Who Was Alex Trebek?

It was nearly seven o'clock in the evening on January 8, 2021. All over the East Coast of the United States, people turned on their televisions. It was time for *Jeopardy!*—a game show that tests the players' knowledge in all sorts of areas from geography to history to pop culture to words that begin and end in a vowel.

Many *Jeopardy!* fans didn't just watch the contestants on the show; they also played along at home. Sometimes they played against each other. If they were watching alone, they just shouted out the answers to themselves.

Tonight's episode was very special. For thirty-seven years, the show had been hosted by Alex Trebek. This episode was his last. Alex had taped this final show months earlier, on October 29,

2020. He was very sick with cancer and could no longer work. Just a week after that, on November 8, 2020, Alex died. So, his fans were watching his last episode, knowing that they would never see him again.

The show's familiar theme music started. A spinning globe filled the screen. Then Johnny Gilbert, the show's announcer, declared, "This is *Jeopardy!*"

Johnny introduced the day's contestants. One was an assistant professor of English education from New York named Jim Gilligan. The next was a software engineering manager from Illinois named Cliff Chang. The third contestant was the returning champion. She had won the previous two days' games. She was an executive assistant from California. Her name was Yoshie Hill. In the two days she had been on the show she had won $31,600.

When he finished introducing the contestants,

Johnny said, "And now, here is the host of *Jeopardy!*, Alex Trebek!"

On this evening, the applause was even longer than usual. At the start of the episode, Alex asked everyone watching at home to be generous with each other. "We're trying to build a gentler, kinder society," he said. "If we all pitch in just a little bit, we're going to get there." Over the years, the audience had grown to love how Alex was always kind to contestants, making them feel good even when they lost the game. Everyone sitting in the audience and watching at home was going to miss seeing Alex on TV every evening. He was more than a television host; he had become part of their lives.

CHAPTER 1
Life on the Nickel Range

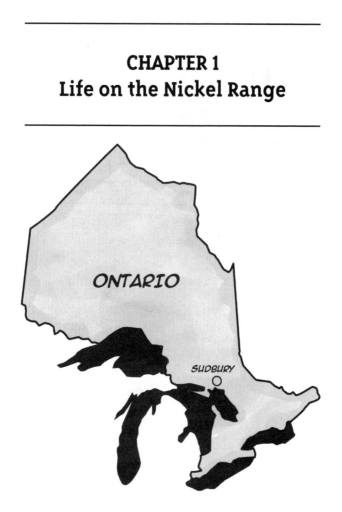

ONTARIO

SUDBURY

On July 22, 1940, George Alexander Trebek was born in Sudbury, Ontario, Canada. Since he had the same first name as his father, his family called him Sonny. As he grew up, he preferred to use his middle name, Alex. Alex's father was born in Ukraine, a country in Eastern Europe. When he moved to Canada, he changed his name from Terebeychuck to Trebek because it was easier for English-speakers to pronounce. Alex's mother, Lucille, was from Canada. Like many Canadians, her first language was French. Alex's father spoke several Eastern European languages, including Ukrainian, Russian, and Polish, so Alex grew up hearing different languages all around him, and he learned to speak two of them—English and French—fluently.

The town of Sudbury is in the Sudbury Basin, the third-largest crater on Earth. It was created when a comet hit Ontario 1 billion 850 million years ago. The comet scattered valuable metals like copper and gold all throughout the basin. People came from all over, especially

Eastern Europe, to work in the mines there. Sudbury became known as the nickel capital of the world.

Workers at the Podolsky Mine in the Sudbury Basin

Alex's father worked as a cook at the Nickel Range Hotel. Alex often got to sit in the hotel's kitchen while his father cooked. Sometimes he was given little jobs to do, like cutting slices out of the big sheet cakes they served in the dining room.

French Canada

Although many people think of Canada as an English-speaking country, according to the 2016 census, French is the native language of around 7.2 million Canadians—that's about 20 percent of all Canadians.

In 1534, a French explorer named Jacques Cartier arrived at the shores of Newfoundland,

French explorer Jacques Cartier

in what is now northeastern Canada. He was looking for a more direct route to Asia. He claimed the country for France, and the French made settlements there throughout the seventeenth century. In the eighteenth century, the country came under British rule, but there are still French speaking areas there today, especially in the province of Quebec, where French is the official language.

When Alex was two, his sister, Barbara, was born. Alex took being a big brother seriously. One day when Alex was seven, he saw his five-year-old sister playing with some friends on the frozen river near their house. He scolded them for playing on the ice. If the river was not completely frozen, they could fall into the freezing water. To make sure it was safe, Alex

tested the ice himself. He took a few steps. The ice beneath him cracked. Alex fell into the water. He splashed around desperately, trying to swim back to shore, but he couldn't even tell where the shore was. The water carried him away across the river! He was pulled out by a passing railway worker who walked him back home, soaking wet.

There were two elementary schools in Sudbury. One of them taught all their classes in English. The other taught mostly in French. Alex decided to go to the French school, and so did many of his friends.

When Alex was nine, his mother got sick with tuberculosis, a contagious disease that affected her lungs. She had to go away to live in a hospital for more than a year. Alex missed her, but he and Barbara still had their father, as well as their grandparents, who also lived in town. And Alex had a lot of friends. They played sports after school, including hockey, baseball, basketball, and football.

After Alex's mother returned from the hospital, the family moved into a new house, which his parents had been saving for. Alex liked his new home. His father converted the porch into a long bedroom for Alex and his sister to share. Alex was a good student, but when he was in seventh grade, he had trouble with a teacher, Mrs. Jennings. Mrs. Jennings didn't like Alex's handwriting because it slanted to the left. Good handwriting, she said, should slant to the right.

When Alex's writing leaned the wrong way, Mrs. Jennings slapped his hands.

Alex went home and told his parents, "I'm not going back to Mrs. Jennings's class."

Alex transferred to the English-speaking school. The students at that school were not very welcoming to a boy who had come from the French school. So, after two months, Alex returned to his French school. He even came back to Mrs. Jennings's class. She never complained about his handwriting again.

Alex was glad to be back in his old school. He was also discovering something new to love: the radio. At night in his bedroom, he often lay in bed listening to broadcasts. Alex's radio was small but powerful. It picked up stations from faraway cities like Boston, Massachusetts, in the United

States. Alex especially liked listening to shows called *The Great Gildersleeve* and *Suspense*.

CHAPTER 2
On His Way

When Alex got older, he became friends with a boy named Maurice Rouleau, whose father owned the Nickel Range Hotel. Maurice was a year older than Alex. In 1954, when Alex was in ninth grade, Maurice went away to an all-boys boarding school. Alex asked his parents if he could go to that school, too. So, the following year he joined Maurice at the University of Ottawa prep school.

That same year, Alex's parents told him they were getting a divorce. His mother moved to Detroit, Michigan, where her sisters, Alex's aunts, lived. Alex was angry and upset about his parents splitting up and his mother being more than four hundred miles away. It wasn't the first time Alex

had been separated from his mother. But when she went to the hospital, Alex knew she was coming back. Now she was starting a new life in a different country. His parents sold their house, and Alex's father moved to a smaller apartment in Sudbury.

Alex's anger showed in his schoolwork. Although he still liked playing sports at school, his grades dropped, and he didn't pay attention in class. At the end of the school year, he was told that he should not return to the University of Ottawa prep school the next semester.

That summer at home, Alex started to regret not behaving well at school. His father thought he deserved another chance. So, the two of them drove together from Sudbury to Ottawa. Once there, Alex's father begged the principal to let Alex return. He said yes. Alex made sure that the principal never regretted that decision.

Alex graduated from Ottawa prep in 1957. He hoped to go to college at the University of Ottawa. He didn't have money to pay for the school, so he applied to the ROTP, or the Regular Officer Training Program. This was a program run by the Canadian Armed Forces.

Canadian
Armed Forces logo

If he was accepted to the program, the government would pay for Alex to go to college. In exchange, he would serve in the Canadian military for two years.

Alex spent two days being tested at an air force base in London, Ontario. Three weeks later, he received his results. He did so well on the test, he was ordered to report to the Royal Canadian Air Force Academy college in Saint-Jean, Quebec. But Alex was very unhappy. He didn't want to go to a military college six hundred miles away from home.

As soon as Alex reported to the Air Force Academy, he knew he didn't like it. He was told what to wear and how to cut his hair. It was a tradition for older students to order the new students around and play tricks on them. Alex didn't like that at all. So, he went to the vice commandant, who was in charge, and told him he was leaving. "Don't worry, Sonny," Alex's father said when Alex returned home on the train. "Everything will be all right."

Back in Sudbury, Alex first lived in a tiny room in the hotel for a while, then moved in with his mother's brother and his wife, because they had an extra room where Alex could stay. He still didn't have money for college, but in Canada, students could return to high school for an extra year that counted as a first year of college. So, Alex returned to Sudbury High, where he had spent ninth grade.

Sudbury Secondary School in Ontario

Alex's room at his aunt and uncle's house was barely big enough for a bed and a desk. But he still made room for his little radio that he loved. He often recorded his favorite shows and songs. There was only one thing Alex didn't like about the radio. He disliked how the disc jockeys, or DJs—people who play prerecorded music to an audience—would talk over the

beginnings of songs. His uncle Ben would laugh every time he heard Alex yelling at the radio, "Shut up! I want the whole song!"

Alex had grown up loving all sorts of shows, not just the ones that played music. He hoped to become a radio announcer, producing and hosting shows on all sorts of topics. He applied for a job at a local radio station. The station manager said he was too young to be an announcer, but that he had a very nice voice. Alex wasn't discouraged. He knew he would try again one day.

CHAPTER 3
Learning on Live TV

Alex applied and was accepted to the University of Ottawa in 1958. Since he did not have a scholarship to pay for school, he worked part-time jobs to make money. Most of the jobs weren't very interesting to him, like when he processed tax forms for the Canadian Revenue Agency.

His jobs still left Alex time to play sports. He played baseball and football. Alex wasn't the strongest player on any team. What he was best at was encouraging the rest of the team. If they were losing a game, Alex could always keep them from giving up.

When Alex was older and in his junior year, he tried out for another job as an announcer at

a radio station. He didn't get the job, but that summer he worked for the Canadian Broadcasting Corporation. He worked there again during his Christmas break. The station liked him so much that in his last year of college they offered him a job as a staff announcer. In the morning, Alex reported on things like the current price of cattle. In the afternoon, he went to class.

Alex graduated from the university in 1961. He continued to work at the station in Ottawa for two years. Then the CBC transferred him to its headquarters in Toronto. Alex was the only bilingual announcer on staff there, reporting in both English and French. He also became the host of a weekly TV show for teenagers called *Music Hop*.

Through the show, Alex met popular singers. He also got his first taste of being a celebrity. People sometimes stopped him on the street to tell him how much they liked the show. The most important thing that Alex learned from that show was how to not take himself too seriously. *Music Hop* was filmed live. That meant that the show wasn't recorded, then broadcasted later. People would watch the show as it happened. Everyone makes mistakes sometimes on live TV. When that happened, Alex just had to go on with the show. He learned quickly to laugh at his own mistakes.

While Alex was still hosting *Music Hop*, he was given another show to host. This one was a quiz show called *Reach for the Top*. The contestants were all teenagers. Most of them had never been on TV before. They were nervous and would be embarrassed if they made a mistake. Alex noticed that sometimes one mistake could

Contestants from *Reach for the Top*, 1960s

ruin the whole game for a contestant. It was tough for Alex to see that happen. So, he used the encouragement skills he'd learned playing sports. Instead of saying, "That's wrong," he would say something like, "You were so close!" It made a difference.

In 1967, Canada celebrated its centennial.

The country was one hundred years old. Since Alex was the only bilingual announcer, he was chosen to host a two-hour variety show with lots of performers. Even Queen Elizabeth II of England would be there!

After the show was over, everyone lined up to meet Queen Elizabeth II and her husband, Prince Philip. Usually, the queen shook a person's hand quickly and said, "Please tell me your name and where you are from" before moving to the next person. But when she got to Alex, she continued to chat with him for a few minutes.

This was because Prince Philip had stopped to talk to someone else and she was waiting for him.

That night all of Alex's friends called him. "The queen must have really liked you," they all said. "We saw how long she spoke with you." Alex felt very flattered.

The very next day, he hosted another show at a football stadium. The queen was there, too. After that show, Alex was eager to talk to her again. He reached out his hand to greet her and the queen said, "Please tell me your name and where you're from."

She didn't remember him at all! But Alex was a good sport about it.

Queen Elizabeth II (1926–2022)

Queen Elizabeth II was the older daughter of King George VI of England. When he died in February 1952, Elizabeth, who was only twenty-five years old, became queen of the United Kingdom. She also became the queen of Canada, because Canada is part of the British Commonwealth. She and her husband, Prince Philip, had four children: Charles, Anne, Andrew, and Edward.

In 2017, Elizabeth celebrated her Sapphire Jubilee, or sixty-five years on the throne. In 2022, she celebrated her Platinum Jubilee, or seventieth anniversary as the ruler of the United Kingdom, and became the first British monarch to do so.

When Queen Elizabeth II passed away on September 8, 2022, at the age of ninety-six, her son Charles became king—King Charles III. At the time of her death, Elizabeth was the longest-living and longest-reigning British monarch, as well as the longest-serving female head of state in history.

CHAPTER 4
Hello, Los Angeles

In 1974, an educational television network in the province of Ontario started producing a show called *Witness to Yesterday*, where celebrities pretended to be famous historical figures who were being interviewed by a host. Alex was thrilled when he was offered a chance to play the American writer Mark Twain. Mark Twain was one of Alex's favorite authors. Most "guests" were on the show for only one episode, but Alex knew so much about Mark Twain

Alex as Mark Twain

that he was interviewed in costume as the great author for two episodes. He didn't even need to use a script.

A year earlier, Alex got a call from Alan Thicke, a Canadian actor, singer, and writer who also hosted game shows in Ontario. Alex had met Alan when Alex interviewed him during an afternoon variety show. He was

Alan Thicke

now working in Los Angeles, a city in California, where many TV shows and movies are produced.

Alan was writing for a new game show in the United States called *The Wizard of Odds*, and it needed a host. "Would you be interested?" Alan asked.

"Sure!" Alex said. He flew to New York City,

rehearsed all day, and did a practice round with contestants before flying back to Toronto that evening. Alan called him that same night. He had gotten the job.

The Wizard of Odds was going to premiere in July 1973, and Alex would need to move to Los Angeles to film it. His sister, Barbara, was already living there. Before moving to California, Alex decided to grow a mustache. He was the first game show host on television with a mustache since Groucho Marx in the 1950s on *You Bet Your Life*.

Alex as the host of *The Wizard of Odds*

Alex with Elaine Callei, 1970s

There was one person in Canada that Alex did not want to leave behind. Elaine Callei had been the host of a show called *Call Callei*. The two had met in Toronto in the early 1970s while Alex was hosting shows there, and they fell in love. Elaine had a six-year-old daughter named Nicky. Soon after Alex moved to Los Angeles, Elaine and Nicky moved there, too. Alex and Elaine got married in 1974.

The Wizard of Odds involved a lot of numbers and math. As the host, Alex had to keep them all straight. Once, in a bonus round, a contestant playing for a new car lost. "That's too bad," Alex started to say. But he had been adding up the players' points in his head as they went along. "Wait a minute, the math doesn't work! *We* made a mistake." Alex wasn't sure what to do. It didn't

seem fair to the player. Alex said, "You shouldn't be punished for our mistake. So, I'm going to give you the car anyway." The audience went wild. Alex thought he'd done the right thing. But his boss, the executive producer, didn't agree. "Next time," he said, "we'll just stop the tape. Don't give the car away."

Alex was enjoying his new life in Los Angeles.

Elaine suggested that Alex's mother could come and live with them, too. She moved into the guesthouse on their property.

The Wizard of Odds only lasted a year on TV, but Alex quickly got another job hosting a show called *High Rollers*. *High Rollers* was a much easier show to host. There wasn't a lot of math.

Alex hosts *High Rollers*

Alex's cohosts and the players just rolled giant dice. The show lasted for two years. During that same time, Alex hosted another game show in Canada called *The $128,000 Question*. That show was filmed in Toronto. Alex had to fly back and forth to tape both shows.

Alex was very busy, but he loved it. Elaine started doing a lot of charity work in Los Angeles, and Nicky had her grandmother at home to take care of her whenever she needed her.

You Bet Your Life

You Bet Your Life was a popular game show that was broadcast on both radio and on television from 1950 to 1961. Contestants were chosen from the audience. They answered a series of questions from different categories. The show was also known for its "secret word," which was revealed to the audience at the start of each show. If a contestant said the word, a toy duck dropped from the ceiling with a $100 prize. The duck wore eyeglasses and a mustache to look like the show's host, Groucho Marx.

Groucho Marx

CHAPTER 5
Introducing Alex Trebel

Alex never turned down work when it was offered. He had seven jobs in ten years. He even hosted one show in Canada where he interviewed people while wearing ice skates! The shows never lasted for very long. Most were quickly forgotten.

But Alex himself was becoming a familiar face. He didn't know how familiar until a friend of his in Canada sent him a video of a popular Canadian comedy show called *SCTV*. The show did a sketch about a game show where actor Eugene Levy played a host called "Alex Trebel" who was obviously based on Alex. He even had Alex's signature mustache. Alex loved it.

ALEX TREBEL

He appreciated having something to laugh about, because his personal life wasn't as happy as it had been. His father was sick with cancer, so the family often traveled to Canada to see him. Back in Los Angeles, Alex's marriage to Elaine was not working out. They still loved each other, but they did not want to be married anymore.

Around that time, Alex was hosting a show in Los Angeles called *Battlestars*. In it, celebrities answered questions about themselves and contestants tried to guess whether or not they were telling the truth. One of the celebrities was a young comedian named Jerry Seinfeld, who went on to have his own very popular TV show, *Seinfeld*.

Battlestars aired in the middle of the day and didn't have a large audience. People just didn't think the game was very fun to watch. At that time, one of the most popular game shows was *Wheel of Fortune*, loosely based on the game of hangman. Contestants guessed consonants and "bought" vowels to try to solve a word puzzle.

Wheel of Fortune

It was created by one of the most successful television hosts and game show creators in the United States, Merv Griffin.

One day in 1980, Alex got a call from the vice president of Merv Griffin's production company. "We're scheduled to tape a *Wheel* tournament this weekend," he said. The host of the show was in the hospital and they needed a replacement fast. Alex's many years of hosting different shows had earned him a good reputation. Merv knew he could count on Alex to do a good job on short notice. Alex stepped in to host the tournament. Merv was pleased with how good he was.

Alex and Elaine got divorced in 1981 and no

longer lived together, but they were still the best of friends. In fact, they bought houses across the street from each other. Alex's mother, Lucille, moved in with Elaine so she could help take care of Nicky while Elaine was at work. In the evenings, she came over to see Alex. He was glad to have his mother with him, especially after his father died of cancer in January 1982. Although Alex missed him, he knew that whatever came next in life, his father would be proud of him, but he couldn't yet imagine just how much his life was about to change.

Merv Griffin (July 6, 1925–August 12, 2007)

Merv Griffin was a TV host and producer. He had his own popular talk show, *The Merv Griffin Show*, which ran from 1969 to 1986. He started his career as a singer on the radio and  later formed his own record label. He performed in movies, but his real fame came when he started hosting a talk show where he interviewed celebrity guests. It won eleven Emmy Awards. He went on to create other shows, including *Wheel of Fortune* and *Jeopardy!* Merv also wrote a little song to be played while the contestants were writing their answers in the final round of *Jeopardy!* The now-famous tune is called "Think!"

CHAPTER 6
This Is *Jeopardy!*

A couple of years after Alex filled in on *Wheel of Fortune*, that show, now hosted by Pat Sajak,

Pat Sajak

went into syndication. That meant that the show was sold to different local channels all across the country that could decide when to put it on. *Wheel* was a half an hour long and usually ran in the evenings. The show's producer, Merv Griffin, wanted to create another show that he could sell with *Wheel of Fortune* to fill an entire hour in the evenings.

He decided to bring back a show that he had produced from 1964 to 1975. It was called *Jeopardy!*, and it tested contestants on their knowledge in different areas of trivia. Instead of contestants answering questions, they were given clues in the form of an answer. Then they had to come up with the question. According to Merv, he got the idea from his wife, Julann.

Jeopardy! episode from the 1970s

Merv remembered what a good job Alex had done when he stepped in to host the tournament on *Wheel of Fortune*. He decided to offer him the job as the new host of the show. The job didn't pay much, so Alex asked Merv if he could also be one of the producers who helped put the show together. Merv agreed.

Alex's first episode aired on September 10, 1984. Not many people watched it. The very first clue selected by a contestant was: "These rodents first got to America by stowing away on ships."

THESE RODENTS
FIRST GOT TO
AMERICA BY
STOWING AWAY
ON SHIPS

The correct response was: "What are rats?" If the contestant did not phrase the response as a question, it didn't count.

Even after several months, *Jeopardy's* audience remained small. One of the distributors trying to sell the program claimed it was because the questions were too hard. Alex promised him that he would make the questions easier, but he didn't actually change them at all.

To raise interest in the show, Alex traveled around the country, appearing on morning shows with Pat Sajak and *Wheel's* cohost, Vanna White. He went along on trips to look for contestants. The show put out an announcement about the search, and people came in to take a fifty-question test. Only people who scored high enough were considered for the show. Sometimes, while the tests were being graded, Alex would go out and talk with the people who hoped to pass the test and be on the show.

Alex, Vanna White, and Pat Sajak during
a morning show appearance

Little by little, the show started to catch on. Viewers at home didn't think the questions were too hard. In fact, they liked challenging themselves by trying to guess the clues from the comfort of their couches.

The little song Merv Griffin had written to play while the contestants thought about their final answers took on a life of its own. When people in everyday life were asked difficult questions, they would often start humming the song while they figured out an answer.

For the first time in his life, Alex had a job that seemed like it was going to last a while. He started thinking about other things he'd like to do in the world.

When Alex began hosting *Jeopardy!* in 1984, the country of Ethiopia in Africa was experiencing a terrible famine. People there were starving. Alex started working with World Vision, a charity that helped people all over the world.

When he wasn't taping the show, he traveled to Ethiopia and other countries that needed help. He didn't go as a TV personality. He just helped distribute things to people who needed them.

Alex with US troops in the 1990s

Alex did perform as a show host with the USO, or United Service Organizations. He visited United States troops who were stationed abroad and invited them to play rounds of *Jeopardy!*

live onstage. He also got involved in protecting animals—especially his favorite, the musk ox. Alex had once read that when musk oxen were threatened by predators, the males formed a circle around the calves and cows, their horns facing out, to protect them. As long as they stood together, they were safe. Alex thought that was a great example to live by.

As *Jeopardy!* got even more popular, the show started running special tournaments. In 1987, they held the first teen tournament for contestants in high school. The following year, they held the first tournament for college students.

Jeopardy! Rules

Jeopardy! has three rounds: Jeopardy!, Double Jeopardy!, and Final Jeopardy! There are six subject categories in each of the first two rounds. Each category has fives "clues," or questions. In the Jeopardy! round, clues are worth $200 up to $1,000. In Double Jeopardy!, clues are worth $400 to $2,000. The clues are given in the form of answers, and contestants must give a reply in the form of a question—or it doesn't count.

After a clue is revealed, the first contestant to hit their buzzer gets to give a response that fits the clue. If they are right, they win the value of that clue and they get to choose the next clue. If they get it wrong, they lose that amount and another contestant gets a chance to answer.

Daily Doubles are hidden on the game board in the first two rounds. They give contestants the chance to earn even more money.

In Final Jeopardy!, there is only a single clue. The contestants are shown the subject category and then place their bets based on that topic.

They are given a clue and thirty seconds to write down their question, which is later revealed on their screen. If they are correct, they get to add that amount to their total score. If they're wrong, they lose that amount. The contestant with the highest score at the end of Final Jeopardy! is the winner and gets to keep the amount of money they've won. They then return to play another game.

Alex enjoyed meeting different people, but he never got to talk much to any of the contestants. The show taped five episodes a day, with only fifteen minutes between each game. Besides, Alex never wanted any contestant to feel like he favored one over the other. He was rooting for all of them.

CHAPTER 7
A World-Famous Mustache

Jeopardy! was filmed in front of a live audience. Alex taped two days a week, five shows a day. In between each show, he changed his suit to make it look like it was a new day. He tried to keep each game a little different. He would never

think about what he was going to say until right before he went on. He always tried to think of a variety of ways to welcome the audience. He might say, "Happy Valentine's Day!" if he knew the show was going to air on TV that day.

During the commercial breaks, Alex would

talk to the audience. Every audience seemed to ask him the same questions: *What's your favorite color?* ("Gray, to match my personality.") *What are your favorite* Jeopardy! *categories?* ("Geography, movies, and movies about geography.") *How would you do as a contestant?* ("A good thirty-year-old would clean my clock.")

In 1988, a friend of Alex's introduced him to a woman named Jean Currivan. Not long after she and Alex started dating,

Jean Currivan

Alex went to Thailand to do some work for World Vision. When he came back, he brought Jean a present: a little bamboo truck. When Jean opened the back of the truck, she found another gift inside: a sapphire and diamond ring. Alex asked her to marry him, and Jean said yes!

They got married in April 1990 at the Regency Club in Westwood, California. At the altar, the minister asked, "Do you, Alex, take Jean to be your wife?"

Alex replied, as if he were hosting the show, "The answer is . . . yes!"

Just three weeks after their wedding, Alex and Jean discovered they were expecting a baby.

Alex with Jean and baby Matthew

Alex's son, Matthew, was born in February 1991, a few months after Alex won his second Outstanding Game Show Host Emmy Award for *Jeopardy!* The Emmy is awarded for excellence in television programming. In 1993, Alex and Jean had a daughter, Emily.

Jeopardy! added a new tournament where celebrities played for charity. It was fun watching stars try to guess answers, but everyone could see that the game had to be made a little easier for them because they hadn't earned their spot the way the actual contestants did. The first celebrity tournament ran on October 26, 1992. The first players were actresses Carol Burnett and Donna Mills and TV host Regis Philbin.

Frank Spangenberg

The real stars of *Jeopardy!* were the everyday people who competed. Some of them really stood out because they answered so many questions correctly. People like Frank Spangenberg, a policeman who won five days in a row. That was the maximum number of days any contestant was allowed to compete. The producers of the show worried that if a person continued to win for more than a week, the audience might start to think that person had an unfair advantage. By the end of his week in 1990, everyone was cheering for Frank. Another big winner was Brad Rutter, who

Brad Rutter

was a college student when he first appeared on *Jeopardy!* He also won five days in a row.

Although Alex didn't think of himself as one of the stars of the show, he was quickly becoming everyone's favorite game show host. He appeared on talk shows like *Late Night with David Letterman.* He also appeared in movies like *White Men Can't Jump* and TV shows including *Cheers, Saturday Night Live,* and *The Golden Girls* as himself. A cartoon version of Alex even appeared on *The Simpsons.*

Alex's face was so familiar that it was a big shock to most of the audience when he decided to

Alex appears as a cartoon in *The Simpsons*

shave his mustache in 2001. By that point, Alex had worn it for almost thirty years. He was about to tape his final show of the day. Sitting in the makeup chair, he just grabbed a razor and shaved it off! Then he walked out onstage.

Back at home, Alex talked to his family for several minutes before saying, "Anyone notice anything different about Dad?" The family was

stunned. Matthew was so shocked, he burst into tears! Reports of Alex shaving his mustache were in newspapers and magazines all over the country. That's how famous he—and his mustache—had become!

CHAPTER 8
Big Winners

In 2003, Alex and the producers of *Jeopardy!* made a big decision to get rid of the five-day rule. The audience had liked rooting for Frank Spangenberg so much that the show's producers wanted to give them a chance to get to know the contestants and root for them for a longer time.

This change set the stage for the show's biggest winners yet. People started to last longer than a week. A taxi driver, student, and bartender named Sean Ryan won six games. A writer named Tom Walsh won seven games. Then, in 2004, Ken Jennings appeared on *Jeopardy!* for almost fifteen weeks in a row. He won seventy-four straight games and more than $2.5 million dollars.

Ken Jennings

This rule change made a difference for Alex, too. Usually, he didn't have any time to get to know contestants. He only really spoke to them for a few minutes during the show, when he asked them a personal question to introduce them to the audience. But Ken was on for so long, that he started to feel like a friend to Alex.

The ratings for the show went up while Ken was on—everyone wanted to see the software engineer who knew all the answers!

Ken finally lost to a real estate agent named Nancy Zerg. When he saw he had lost, Ken gave her a hug. "Congratulations," Alex said to Nancy. "You are indeed a giant killer."

Because Ken had been on the show so long, Alex did something special for him. He invited him back the next day so he could say a real goodbye to the audience who had rooted for him. The following year, the show itself broke a record. It won its twenty-fifth Emmy Award, the most ever won by a game show. It put them in the *Guinness Book of World Records*.

Alex didn't have to wonder if this job was going to disappear. His life seemed very stable. But in 2007, his sister, Barbara, died of breast cancer. Alex and his mother were both with her when she died, along with Barbara's husband, in Los Angeles. Losing his sister made Alex even more grateful for the family he had: his mother, who now lived with him, his wife, and two children.

Alex also still considered his ex-wife, Elaine, and her daughter, Nicky, as part of his family.

The Guinness Book of World Records

The Guinness Book of World Records lists world records of human achievements and extremes of the natural world. It was started when Sir Hugh Beaver, the managing director of the Guinness Brewery, was visiting County Wexford in Ireland

Sir Hugh Beaver

in 1951. He got into an argument over whether the golden plover or the red grouse was the fastest game bird in Europe. He realized it would be handy to have a book where you could look that up. (It was the golden plover.) The first edition was published in 1955 and was a huge hit. In 2021, the sixty-sixth edition of *The Guinness Book of World Records* was published in twenty-three languages. The book is sold in one hundred countries around the world and holds over fifty-eight thousand records in its database.

Elaine had become good friends with Alex's wife, Jean. Elaine was now a businesswoman who had started her own company. In the summers, she gave Matthew and Emily, now in high school, jobs there.

Alex might not have known as many answers as Ken Jennings did on *Jeopardy!*, but he felt like he'd won just as big.

CHAPTER 9
A Different Kind of Jeopardy

One day in 2007, Alex was doing some work around the house. He felt a squeezing, tight pain in his chest. He thought he'd pulled a muscle. Jean insisted he go to the hospital to be sure he was okay. When they got there, the doctor told Alex that he was having a heart attack.

Alex was grateful that Jean had made him go to the hospital. He also said he was glad he hadn't bothered the doctors for nothing!

The public didn't know about Alex's heart attack. He recovered quickly and went back to work. In the summer of 2011, he went to San Francisco to host the National Geographic World Championship, a geography contest for students, that he had been hosting since 1989. The contest was being held at Google headquarters. Jean came with him so they could have a vacation there when the contest was finished.

While he was in San Francisco, Alex woke up in the middle of the night. He saw someone walking past the bed in his hotel room. Was he dreaming? No. He thought it must be Jean, but Jean was sleeping next to him.

Who was in his room?

Alex jumped out of bed. His wallet and

bracelet, which he'd put on the dresser, were missing. He hurried into the hall just in time to see a woman duck into the little room where the ice machine was.

"What were you doing in my hotel room?" he demanded when the woman came out.

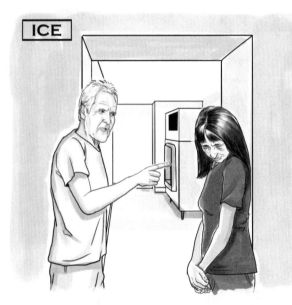

"I wasn't in your hotel room!" she said, but Alex knew she was lying. He was going to call hotel security but the woman took off running.

Alex ran after her. About twenty feet down the hall, something snapped in his foot and he fell. He had torn his Achilles tendon, which attaches the heel of the foot to the calf. Alex limped to a phone to call security.

The woman was arrested. It turned out she had already robbed a lot of people before Alex caught her.

Alex still hosted the competition that day. He was rolled into the auditorium in a wheelchair and used crutches to move around the stage. He joked to the audience that if they shouted out any answers, he would chase them out of the auditorium.

The next year, in June 2012, Alex had a second heart attack. This time he knew to take the squeezing, tight feeling in his chest seriously. Once again, he recovered quickly. He was ready to begin taping *Jeopardy!* again in July.

The audience didn't know about this second heart attack, either. But they noticed right away when Alex grew his mustache back in 2014. He decided to let the viewers vote on whether he should keep it or shave it off again. The audience said: shave it again. Jean was happy because she liked him better without the mustache. That

To 'stache or not to 'stache? That is the question. #AlexTrebek #Jeopardy !

same year, Alex broke the Guinness World Record for hosting the most game show episodes—6,829.

Alex liked getting the audience involved in his life in little ways, like the mustache vote, but he preferred getting to know more about the contestants of the show. In 2016, a forty-one-year-old science content developer from Austin, Texas, really inspired him. Her name was Cindy Stowell and she was a lifelong fan of the show. She won six days in a row. What Alex knew, but the audience and the

Cindy Stowell

other contestants didn't, was that Cindy had stage 4 colon cancer. Stage 4 meant the cancer had spread to other parts of the body, and it was very serious. Cindy knew she didn't have long to live. She had to take breaks during filming because she felt sick.

Cindy's last episode aired on December 21, 2016, but Cindy herself had died on December 5, eight days before her first episode aired. She had won $103,803, which she donated to cancer research.

If Cindy had lived, she would have competed in the show's next Tournament of Champions. That was where past winners competed against each other. So, when the tournament rolled around in 2017, the show made a donation to cancer research for her in her name.

CHAPTER 10
So Long

Alex had been hosting *Jeopardy!* for over three decades, but he still loved doing it. Other things in his life had changed. In 2016, Alex's mother died at age ninety-five. She was living with Alex and his family at the time. But *Jeopardy!* remained the same. It was on every weeknight all over the country. Alex still sometimes found interesting things to suggest as clues for the show. On a trip to England with his family in 2019, Alex visited a little fishing village called Whitby. He learned that this village was the place where Dracula first landed in England in the Bram Stoker novel in which he first appeared. That became a clue in a game that season.

Village of Whitby in England

People were so used to Alex appearing in their living room every night, it was hard to imagine him not being there to introduce the contestants at the beginning of the episodes or to say, "So long!" at the end of each show. But on March 29, 2019, Alex made a sad announcement.

BREAKING NEWS

BREAKING NEWS   "Jeopardy!" host Alex Trebek announces he has stage 4 pancreatic cancer

He had learned that he had pancreatic cancer. It was stage 4. The doctors didn't know how long he would live. Alex only knew that he wanted to keep hosting *Jeopardy!* as long as he could.

Fans of the show all hoped Alex would get well. During the Tournament of Champions that year, a contestant named Dhruv Gaur did not know the answer to the Final Jeopardy! clue. So he decided to use his screen to say something more important. When his answer was revealed, it simply said, "What is, We love you, Alex!"

$5

What is
We ♡ you,
Alex!
$1995

That same year, *Jeopardy!* had another big winner, James Holzhauer. James was an unusual contestant. Normally, players started out with the easier clues in each category and moved up to the harder ones. But James was a professional gambler. He wanted to make as much money as possible. He jumped around the board, choosing all the hardest clues first because they were worth the most money. Alex thought this kind of strategy was a bad idea because it meant contestants were getting the hardest questions before they got familiar with the

James Holzhauer

category. But James, to Alex's surprise, had no trouble answering the hardest questions first.

James won $2,464,216 in thirty-three episodes.

As one of the show's biggest winners, James returned to *Jeopardy!* in 2020 as part of the "Greatest of All Time" Tournament. He played against Brad Rutter and Ken Jennings. Ken ended up winning, but, as always, Alex was rooting for all of them.

As much as Alex wanted to continue to host

the show, his illness made him too weak to continue, and he had to retire. He taped his last show on October 29, 2020, knowing it would not air until January of the next year.

In the year of 2020, the whole country—and most of the world—was forced to spend a lot of time at home to stop the spread of a contagious disease called COVID-19.

Matthew and Emily came to stay with Alex and Jean so their family was together. Matthew now owned two restaurants in New York City. Emily was a real estate agent in California. Alex was no longer strong enough to host the show, but there were plenty of things he could do. He decided he wanted to replace a cloth cover on an outdoor swing in his yard. To do that he had to learn to sew on a portable sewing machine. It took Alex a long time to do it right, and he often had to stop and rest, but when it was finished, he was very proud of his work.

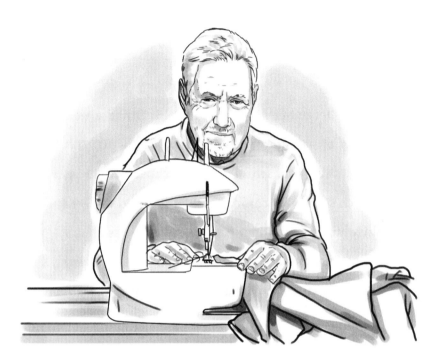

Not long after that, Alex did something else he'd never done before. He sent a text! Even though Alex had a cell phone, he never really felt like he needed to learn new ways to communicate with people.

But one day when he was at home, someone had sent Jean flowers while she was out of the house. He wanted her to see them right away.

COVID-19

In December 2019, scientists identified a new strain of a type of virus called coronavirus. This new strain caused a disease called COVID-19, which stands for coronavirus disease and the year in which it was identified. Because it was a new virus, humans had no immunity to it. It was very contagious and could be spread through the air.

Although some people exposed to the virus didn't show any symptoms, many others became very ill and even died. In March 2020, to keep the virus from spreading, people were told to stay at home as much as possible and wear masks if they went outside. These precautions lasted more than a year. A vaccine that could protect people from the virus was not made available to most adults until April 2021.

So he started looking at the icons on his phone screen, searching for something that looked like a camera. Then for an icon that looked like it would send messages. All by himself, Alex figured out how to take a picture of the flowers on his phone and send it to Jean.

She wrote back, "Look at you, you're texting and sending a picture!" She included a few emojis. Alex didn't know how to send those yet.

Alex died at home with his family on November 8, 2020. He was eighty years old.

Alex's last episode of *Jeopardy!* aired on January 8, 2021. He ended the show with a simple "thank you" to the audience and the words, "We'll see you again next week." Alex had never considered himself the star of the show, so he didn't call any attention to himself with a big goodbye. He just promised the show would be back.

By the time the show aired, the audience knew that Alex had died. The producers of the show followed Alex's last words with clips of Alex and the song "Once Before I Go" playing in the background. The tribute ended with Alex waving and saying, "So long!" to viewers over the years.

Alex Trebek had become an important part of everyone's life without them noticing it. Many were surprised at how sad they were to lose him— much more than they would have predicted. Alex was introduced to people as the host of a revived game show, but soon became a man who was beloved all around the world.

Timeline of Alex Trebek's Life

1940 — George Alexander Trebek is born in Sudbury, Ontario, on July 22

1947 — Falls through the ice of a frozen river near his house

1961 — Gets first professional radio job with the Canadian Broadcasting Corporation

— Graduates from the University of Ottawa

1973 — Moves to Los Angeles

1974 — Marries Elaine Callei

1981 — Divorces Elaine Callei

1984 — Starts hosting *Jeopardy!*

1987 — Goes on the first of thirteen USO tours

1990 — Marries Jean Currivan

1991 — Son Matthew is born

1993 — Daughter Emily is born

2001 — Shaves off his mustache for the first time in almost thirty years

2014 — Enters *The Guinness Book of World Records* for most game show episodes hosted by a presenter

2019 — Announces he has stage 4 pancreatic cancer

2020 — Dies on November 8

Timeline of the World

1941 — The first Captain America comic book is published

1943 — Thomas Jefferson Memorial in Washington, DC, is completed

1947 — Jackie Robinson signs with the Brooklyn Dodgers, becoming the first African American Major League Baseball player since the 1880s

1954 — The movie *Gojira* is released in Japan; its English title is *Godzilla*

1955 — First polio vaccine available in the United States

1958 — The LEGO brick is launched

1982 — The first compact discs (CDs) are produced in Germany

1984 — The Dragon Ball manga series, created by Akira Toriyama, debuts in Japan

1990 — East and West Germany are unified, making Germany a single country again

1994 — The Channel Tunnel, an undersea rail tunnel connecting England and France, opens

2003 — China launches Shenzhou 5 and becomes the third nation to launch a crewed space mission

2010 — Korean pop group BTS first formed

2021 — Kamala Harris becomes the first woman vice president of the United States

Bibliography

*Books for young readers

*Anderson, Kirsten. **Who Is Ken Jennings?** New York: Penguin Workshop, 2021.

Garrand, Danielle. "Alex Trebek's 'Jeopardy!' wardrobe donated to help people who've experienced addiction, homelessness and incarceration go on job interviews." **CBS News**, February 21, 2021. https://www.cbsnews.com/news/alex-trebek-jeopardy-wardrobe-donation-suit/.

Jeopardy! From Academic Kids, Academic Kids Encyclopedia. https://academickids.com/encyclopedia/index.php/Jeopardy%21.

Jeopardy! Teen Tournament Facts for Kids, Kiddle, July 16, 2021. https://kids.kiddle.co/Jeopardy!_Teen_Tournament.

Mazziotta, Julie. "Inside Trebek's Health Battles Throughout His 36 Years on Jeopardy!" **People Magazine**, November 9, 2020. https://people.com/health/alex-trebek-jeopardy-health-battles/.

Puckett, Jane. **Alex Trebek 162 Success Facts: Everything You Need to Know About Alex Trebek.** Brisbane, Australia: Emereo Publishing, 2014.

Trebek, Alex. **The Answer Is . . .: Reflections on My Life.** New York: Simon & Schuster, 2020.